Steve Nash

By Robert Walker

Crabtree Publishing Company

www.crabtreebooks.com

Crabtree Publishing Company

www.crabtreebooks.com

Author: Robert Walker
Publishing plan research and development:
  Sean Charlebois, Reagan Miller
  Crabtree Publishing Company
Project coordinator: Kathy Middleton
Photo research: Crystal Sikkens
Editor: Wendy Scavuzzo
Designer: Ken Wright
Production coordinator and prepress
  technician: Ken Wright
Print coordinator: Katherine Berti

Photographs:
Associated Press: pages 9, 11, 12, 13, 16–17,
  19, 20, 21, 22
Dreamstime: Catabar: page 1; Cedul50: pages
  5, 24
Getty Images: WireImage: pages 6, 26; Jeff
  Vinnick/ NHLI: page 7 (bottom); Sports
  Illustrated: pages 10, 14–15
Keystone Press: ZUMAPRESS.com: cover,
  pages 23, 25
Shutterstock: Debby Wong: page 4
Wikimedia Commons: Hakandahlstrom:
  page 7 (top)

Library and Archives Canada Cataloguing in Publication

Walker, Robert, 1980-
    Steve Nash / Robert Walker.

(Superstars!)
Includes index.
Issued also in electronic formats.
ISBN 978-0-7787-7618-5 (bound).--ISBN 978-0-7787-7631-4 (pbk.)

    1. Nash, Steve, 1974- --Juvenile literature. 2. Basketball
players--Canada--Biography--Juvenile literature. I. Title.
II. Series: Superstars! (St. Catharines, Ont.)

GV884.N37W34 2012   j796.323092   C2012-904371-0

Library of Congress Cataloging-in-Publication Data

Walker, Robert.
    Steve Nash / by Robert Walker.
        p. cm. -- (Superstars!)
    Includes index.
    ISBN 978-0-7787-7618-5 (reinforced library binding) -- ISBN 978-0-7787-7631-4 (pbk.) -- ISBN 978-1-4271-7920-3 (electronic pdf) -- ISBN 978-1-4271-8035-3 (electronic html)
    1. Nash, Steve, 1974---Juvenile literature. 2. Basketball players--Canada--Biography--Juvenile literature. 3. Basketball players--United States--Biography--Juvenile literature. I. Title.

GV994.N37W35 2012
796.323092--dc23
[B]
                                        2012024793

Crabtree Publishing Company

www.crabtreebooks.com   1-800-387-7650

Printed in Canada/102012/MA20120817

Published in Canada
Crabtree Publishing
616 Welland Ave.
St. Catharines, ON
L2M 5V6

Published in the United States
Crabtree Publishing
PMB 59051
350 Fifth Avenue, 59th Floor
New York, New York 10118

Published in the United Kingdom
Crabtree Publishing
Maritime House
Basin Road North, Hove
BN41 1WR

Published in Australia
Crabtree Publishing
3 Charles Street
Coburg North
VIC 3058

CONTENTS

Words that are defined in the glossary are in
bold type the first time they appear in the text.

Meet Steve Nash

Skills to Pay the Bills

There are ten seconds left on the game clock. The Suns are down by two. The hometown Phoenix crowd is on its feet, filling the rafters of US Airways Center with shouts and cheers. The ball is inbound to Suns' star **point guard** Steve Nash. The **NBA** veteran is exhausted. Up ahead he can see the defense getting ready to put a double team in his way. Steve starts to dribble, while scanning the court for an open man.

Most people would find this overwhelming, but not Steve Nash. This is the kind of high-pressure game he thrived on for ten years with the Phoenix Suns, and the reason the Los Angeles Lakers wanted him so badly. As a point guard, Steve acts as the quarterback for his team. He is in control of the ball as the offense moves up the court. He calls the plays and decides whether to pass the ball or take it to the net himself. A point guard must be an excellent shooter, passer, and ball handler.

A Winner on and off the Court

Steve has earned a lot of awards during his basketball career. He led several championship teams in high school and university, as well as set club records for assists and shooting. Since his rookie year in the NBA 1996–1997 season, Steve has won the league's Most Valuable Player award twice and has been chosen for the all-star game an impressive eight times. While he may not have the height or flashiness of other NBA stars, Steve is known for his work ethic and dedication which have helped him climb to the top of the NBA ladder.

HELPING CHILDREN

Steve is involved with many charities that help people in need. He even has his own children's charity called the Steve Nash Foundation.

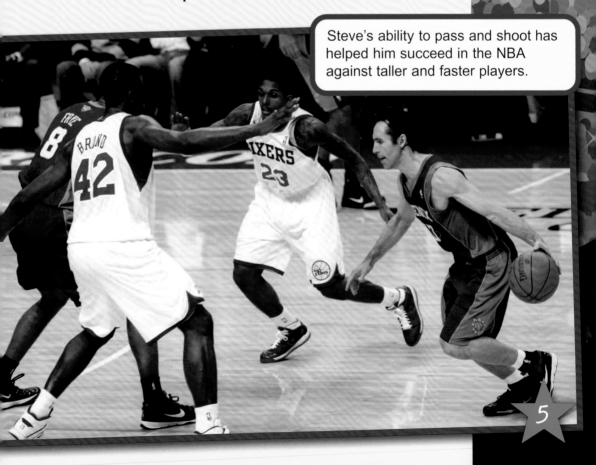

Steve's ability to pass and shoot has helped him succeed in the NBA against taller and faster players.

The Early Years

The Steve Nash story began all the way on the other side of the world in South Africa. Born in 1974 in the city of Johannesburg, Steve grew up in a soccer household. In fact, Steve's dad John was a semiprofessional soccer player. When Steve was just two years old, his parents decided to move to Canada. At the time, South Africa was controlled by an **apartheid** government, which mistreated anyone who wasn't white. Steve's parents didn't want to bring up their children under such unfair conditions. They eventually settled in Victoria, British Columbia. It was there that Steve had a typical Canadian upbringing, learning how to play hockey, lacrosse, basketball, and baseball.

John Nash

It Runs in the Family

Steve was a natural when it came to sports and so were the other Nash children. Steve, his brother Martin, and their sister Joann all inherited their dad's love for soccer. Steve left the soccer pitch for basketball, but his brother Martin continued to play and eventually made it into pro teams in the United States and Canada. Sister Joann Nash was captain of the University of Victoria women's soccer team for three years.

Ice Dreams

Like most of his friends, one of Steve's early sports heroes was NHL legend Wayne Gretzky. Steve admired the Great One's abilities as a playmaker. Gretzky had an uncanny ability to read the action around him, finding open teammates to pass to or taking the puck in by himself. Believe it or not, young Steve Nash's early dreams were of becoming a professional athlete on the ice—not the basketball court. Basketball wasn't as popular as hockey was in Canada. But as high school approached, Steve made the decision to focus on basketball as his sport of choice. He would adopt Gretzky's skill at making things happen on the ice and carry it over to the basketball court.

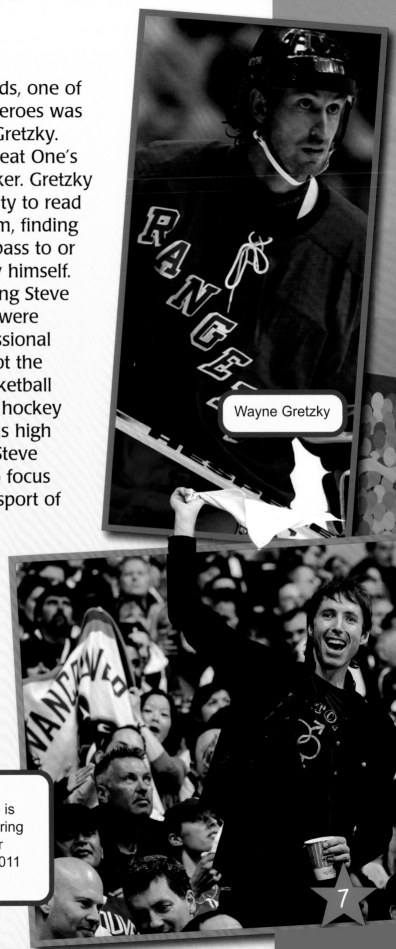

Wayne Gretzky

Steve still enjoys hockey today. He is shown here cheering for the Vancouver Canucks in the 2011 **NHL** playoffs.

7

Focus on the Court

Teenage Steve gave 100 percent to basketball. He still enjoyed soccer and other sports, but basketball became his passion. He played for the Mount Douglas High School basketball team and was chosen as most valuable player as a junior.

Balancing Books and Basketball

Steve moved to a different school during his fourth year of high school. While he was excelling in sports and winning at chess, Steve's schoolwork was suffering. He just wasn't making the time to stay on top of his schoolwork. Steve's parents saw that something had to be done to keep Steve's grades on par with his athletics. They wanted their son to continue his education after graduating high school. So the decision was made to enroll Steve at St. Michaels University School in Victoria, British Columbia. St. Michaels was known for helping students excel at sports as well as academically.

Starting Out at St. Michaels

According to the high school transfer rules at the time, Steve would have to sit out from basketball for the year. This was frustrating for Steve, not being able to compete in the sport he loved, but the time off gave Steve a chance to bring up his grades. Steve hit the books with a vengeance. He also spent all of his spare time practicing so he would be ready for the next year's season.

Blue Jags

The St. Michaels coaches were impressed by the new addition to their Blue Jags basketball team. Steve showed star potential his first year on the court, helping the team to the provincial title as well as being picked as top player in all of British Columbia. Steve averaged 21 points, 11 **assists**, and 9 **rebounds** per game. Steve also tried out for the Canadian Junior team while at St. Michaels. The national team competed at the World Championships in Edmonton. Steve didn't make the starting **lineup**, but he was picked as an alternate.

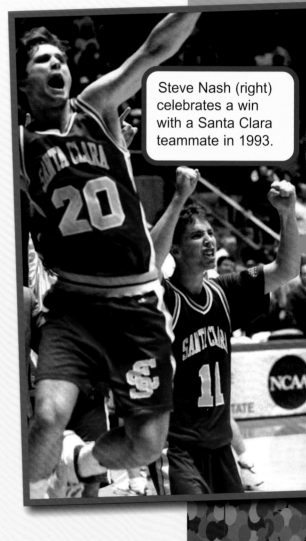

Steve Nash (right) celebrates a win with a Santa Clara teammate in 1993.

Getting Noticed

More than anything, Steve wanted to play university basketball in the United States. Playing for an American school would help Steve's chances of one day making it to the NBA. Also, schools in the United States can offer scholarships to students, which would help Steve's family with the cost of post-secondary schooling. But even with all of Steve's accomplishments at the high school level, he had great difficulty attracting interest from American schools. With the help of his parents and St. Michaels coach Ian Hyde-Lay, he finally got a break when Santa Clara University offered him a scholarship starting in the 1992–1993 season.

Becoming a Bronco

Santa Clara coach Dick Davey was surprised no other American schools had swooped in to grab Steve yet. He was quick to make the trip to Victoria to extend an invitation to make Steve a Bronco. When Steve made the move to sunny California, he became one of a small number of Canadian athletes to play for an American school. It was a big step for Steve, moving far away from his family and friends.

Luckily Steve's upbeat personality made it easy for him to make new friends at the Santa Clara campus. As a rookie, Steve had to work for a place in the Broncos' lineup. Steve increased his already impressive work ethic. When he wasn't in class, he practiced whenever he had a spare moment. Most evenings after school, Steve could be found in the gym practicing his shooting.

MEETING A HERO

In his senior year, Steve met one of his basketball heroes—Magic Johnson. Magic was impressed by Steve's skills and gave him an autograph signed "From Big Magic to Little Magic."

Steve was often seen dribbling a tennis ball around campus to get in some extra practice.

Taking Charge

Santa Clara was a relatively small school compared to others in the **NCAA**. It didn't have the basketball history of universities such as Duke and Indiana, so Santa Clara rarely attracted outstanding athletes. This meant, for the Broncos to win, the players would have to out-hustle and outthink the competition. This gelled perfectly with the sport philosophy of Steve. Steve led Santa Clara to the NCAA finals twice over the next three years. He was also given the West Coast Conference player-of-the-year award twice. By the time Steve had finished at Santa Clara, he had the school record for assists.

Steve was the leader in scoring and assists for the Broncos.

He Said It

"Use every opportunity you have to practise the fundamental skills. Dedicate yourself to working every day on your footwork, your ball handling and dribbling, your passing and catching, your shooting and rebounding. I also believe it's important to practise each position, offensive and defensive, and to always know what to look for when you're on the court."
—*Basketball Basics: How to Play Like the Pros* by Jay Triano and Steve Nash (2009)

In the Big Leagues

Steve was very nervous about his chances going into the 1996 NBA **Draft**. Some NBA scouts had already dismissed Steve, saying he wasn't good enough to play in the big leagues. So when he was picked 15th overall in the very first round of the draft, no one was more surprised and relieved than Steve.

Going Fast

The call to draft Steve was made by Phoenix Suns assistant coach Danny Ainge. Steve had been the top choice for the Suns, and both Ainge and the coaching staff were relieved he wasn't taken by another team in the first round. By being chosen 15th overall in the first round Steve became the highest drafted Canadian player in NBA history. He celebrated with his group of supporters at the Continental Arena. But not everyone was so pleased with the Sun's newest acquisition.

Steve Nash shows his enthusiasm as he becomes the newest member of the Phoenix Suns.

Mixed Feelings

Miles away at the America West Arena in Phoenix, Arizona, Suns fans had gathered to watch the NBA Draft. Many Phoenix fans expressed disappointment with Steve being chosen in such a prime draft position. There was even booing and shouts toward the big screen at America West Arena. The

NBA DRAFT

LIVINGSTON — LONG — MARBURY — MCCARTY — MCCOLLUM — MCCULLOU

MCINNIS — MEEKS — MIGLINIEKS — MILLARD — MINOR — NASH

disgruntled fans argued that there were players with more talent who would have made better draft picks for the Suns franchise. There was also the matter of the Suns current lineup. The Suns already had two talented point guards—NBA stars Jason Kidd and Kevin Johnson. Johnson, who was already a veteran, had agreed to stay on in Phoenix. This had many Suns fans questioning the need for another point guard.

The 1996 NBA Draft was considered by many to be one of the most talented lineups in NBA history.

He Said It

"I probably would've booed myself too, but I'm going to be a really good player and I'm going to help the team a lot. I have a lot of faith in myself and hopefully they'll enjoy watching me play. They want to win and I wouldn't want fans who just sat back and didn't care, so I'm excited to be in a passionate city."
—Interview in "The Canadian Kid" in *Fastbreak* Magazine (Sept./Oct. 1996)

Steve the Underdog

Hearing of his less-than-positive reception during the draft, Steve promised himself and the Suns fans that he would do his best to prove them wrong. Steve's time in Phoenix would be very trying for the rookie. There were a lot of players with more experience ahead of him, and there are only five places to play on the court. Steve also had to contend with the cool reaction from the hometown Phoenix crowd. There were even occasions when Steve would be showered with boos when he took the court.

Riding the Pine

Steve only started in one game during his first season with the Phoenix Suns. He spent a lot of time on the bench, only coming into the game when one of the other players needed a rest. This was quite the change for Steve, but it drove him to practice even harder during exhibition games and in training camp.

Steve didn't get much time on the court during his first season, but when he did he gave it everything he had.

Stiff Competition

NBA basketball was a whole new level of playing. Steve knew he would have to step up his game to survive. In the pros, players were bigger and stronger, the season was longer, and there was a lot more traveling compared to Steve's time in high school and university. As a playmaker, Steve had to change his style of play to meet the pace of the NBA. He had to be faster and better at anticipating the competition. Steve also had to learn all of the Suns' plays, which was very difficult.

Making the Most of Things

Even with a season destined for the bench, Steve made the most of every opportunity. An early injury to starter Kevin Johnson gave Steve more chances to play during training camp and pre-season play. He used these chances to try to impress his coaches and teammates. Many of the Suns veterans saw potential in Steve, and he graciously accepted their constructive criticisms and encouragement. Steve enjoyed the experience of being in the NBA and all of its **perks**, including meeting NBA players and seeing the rest of the country on road games.

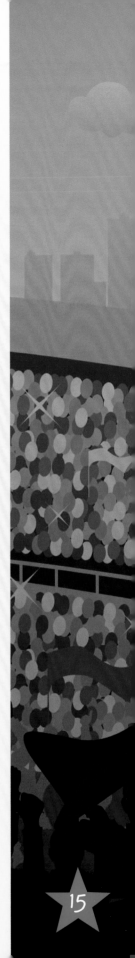

On the Court

In his first home game for the Suns, Steve scored 8 points including a three-pointer and an assist. He averaged around 10 minutes on the court, 3.3 points, 2.1 assists per game. Steve only played about 15 minutes over the course of the playoffs that year. He worked hard on and off the court, slowly winning over the hometown crowd and becoming a fan favorite.

In Front of the Hometown Crowd

The highlight of Steve's tough rookie season was his first game back in his native province of British Columbia. The Phoenix Suns were on the road for a game against the Vancouver Grizzlies. Dozens of friends and family rushed to get tickets to the game. This was a big deal for Steve, so the owner of the Grizzlies gave his parents courtside seats for the game. There was a press conference held especially for the occasion. Steve's teammates good-naturedly teased him about all the attention. Steve played that night, spending over 40 minutes on the court, earning 17 points, 12 assists, and 7 rebounds.

The Second Season

Things began to improve for Steve in his second NBA season with the Phoenix Suns. His time on the floor almost doubled from the last season. This meant more opportunities to contribute to the team. Coach Ainge had so much faith in Steve that the Suns adopted a three-guard rotation, giving all three of the team's point guards equal playing time. Steve went on to average 9.1 points and 3.4 assists per game. He also played over 50 minutes in the playoffs, averaging 5.5 points and 1.8 assists per game. Steve was coming into his own as a player and as a leader on the court. But, while he was beginning to make a name for himself in Phoenix, it seemed to Steve that there wasn't enough room for him to grow as a player with the Suns.

Steve quickly earned a reputation as an excellent shooter and passer.

A Change of Scenery

Steve was developing as a talented player. He was looking for an opportunity to lead a team of his own, but the Suns already had their two veteran point guards. After his second year with Phoenix, Steve started looking at other NBA teams. He eventually was picked up by Dallas, in exchange for Martin Muursepp, Charles "Bubba" Wells, and two draft picks.

BAD BACK

Back problems have followed Steve throughout his career. He often lies on the floor next to the bench to relieve the pain.

On the Rebound

The Dallas Mavericks were a struggling team. The Mavericks had enjoyed success in the 1980s. But, as the decade came to an end, they found themselves plummeting in league standings. In the 1992–1993 and 1993–1994 seasons, Dallas had won only 23 games in total. They had missed the playoffs for eight straight seasons, and the organization and the city of Dallas were desperate to turn things around. New head coach Don Nelson helped get things started by bringing in some fresh players. The team had big hopes for Nash and were willing to sign him to an impressive six-year, $33 million contract.

He Said It

"I felt really at home in Phoenix. I naively felt a lot of loyalty. And you know it's not a business that's built on loyalty. So, I was a little disappointed because I'd really made friends and fit in and felt good there and enjoyed everyone in the organization. But at the end of the day it's about your career. If you don't look out for your career, no one else really is going to."
—*Steve Nash: The Making of an MVP by Jeff Rud* (2007)

A Rough Start

Steve again had to put up with boos and heckling from the fans his first year with the Mavericks. Unfortunately for Steve, his play suffered. This was made worse by a series of injuries to Steve's ankle and nose, on top of an ongoing back condition. Steve missed the last ten games of his first season with injuries. He also went through a nasty shooting slump. At one point, Steve was hitting only 35 percent from the floor. He had a low 7.9 points per game and only 5.5 assists. Steve was just as upset with his playing as the fans were, and he struggled with the pressure.

The Dallas fans gave Steve a hard time his first season with the Mavericks.

The Making of a Legend

Steve had the support of his family, teammates, and even players from other teams during his difficult start with Dallas. The first years for Steve in Dallas were rebuilding years for the team. With hard work and determination, Steve and the team slowly began to improve, win more games, and increase their chances at being in the playoffs.

The Big Three

Things began to fall into place for Steve and the Mavericks in the 2000–2001 season. The team finished the season with a wins/losses record of 53–29 for the year. They also finally made it back to the playoffs. Much of the success was due to Steve's efforts, but he also had the help of two other players in particular. Veteran Michael Finley and German player Dirk Nowitzki joined Steve and they became known as the Big Three—the driving force behind the Mavericks' offense.

Known as the Big Three, Steve Nash (left), Dirk Nowitzki (center), and Michael Finley (right) were an unstoppable force for the Mavericks.

Breaking Stride

Steve was fast becoming a driving force in the NBA. In the 2001–2002 season, Steve racked up 17.9 points and 7.7 assists per game. Even more impressively, his three-point average rose to a whopping 45.5 percent. Steve became more confident and aggressive on the court, taking the reins of the Dallas offense. He helped the Mavericks to a 57–25 season. In the 2002–2003 season Dallas opened with 14 straight wins, going on to finish with their first 60-win season. Steve averaged 17.7 points and 7.3 assists per game. He also broke the franchise record for free throws. In the playoffs, the Mavericks made it all the way to the third round conference finals.

FAMOUS LOCKS

One of Steve's most famous characteristics is his hairstyle. As Steve's reputation in the NBA grew, so did the media's attention on his hair. When he cut his hair, newspapers and magazines ran articles about it!

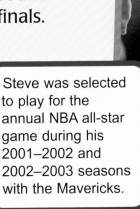

Steve was selected to play for the annual NBA all-star game during his 2001–2002 and 2002–2003 seasons with the Mavericks.

Oh Canada!

One of Steve's proudest moments was being selected to lead Team Canada in the 2000 Summer Olympics in Sydney, Australia. Steve helped the underdog Canadian team through the qualifying tournaments. Only two spots were available to teams from North, South, and Central America. The United States was a sure thing for one slot, leaving the other eight countries to fight over the remaining opening. Canada surprised everyone by making it to the final game against the talented team from Puerto Rico. With the pressure on, Steve led Canada to an 83–71 win with 26 points.

Steve was awarded MVP in the qualifying tournament for the 2000 Summer Olympics.

He Said It

"It was amazing. It was one of the best experiences of my career. It may be the best experience of my career, I don't know. First of all, the Olympics speak for themselves. They are one of those great parts of sports. It was something I always really, really wanted to be a part of."

—Steve Nash: The Making of an MVP by Jeff Rud (2007

Team Player

Even though Steve was an NBA pro player, he didn't demand any special treatment. He traveled and lived with the other players during the Olympics. Steve even gave up his first-class ticket on the plane ride over so one of his taller teammates could enjoy more leg room. Steve was praised by his coaches for being such a hard-working player, even leading drills during team practices.

SHARING THE WEALTH

Because Team Canada was on a tight budget, Steve anonymously donated $3000 to each player so they could enjoy themselves while in Australia.

Olympic Play

At the Olympics, Canada pulled off impressive victories over Yugoslavia, Russia, Australia, and Spain. They were finally defeated by France, after Steve was triple-teamed by the French defense. Canada finished with a 5–2 record.

Steve was also involved in the 2010 Winter Olympics in Vancouver, British Columbia. He was one of Canada's torchbearers that helped light the Olympic flame at the opening ceremony.

23

Signs of Change

After the 2003–2004 season, Steve's contract with Dallas had come to an end. He was a huge part of the Mavericks' offense, and the fans loved him, but Steve had become a hot commodity in the NBA. Mavericks owner Mark Cuban offered Steve a $9 million contract for four years. Unfortunately, this wasn't enough to keep Steve in Dallas. Steve decided to sign with the Phoenix Suns, who offered him $63 million over six years.

Meanwhile, in Phoenix...

After leaving the Mavericks, Steve spent eight years with the Phoenix Suns.

Steve was sad to leave Dallas, but he was also excited to return to the team where he had started his NBA career. Phoenix fans were excited to have Steve back as well. The team was coming off a rough year. They had won only 29 games and had missed the playoffs. Steve helped turn the team around in the 2004–2005 season. The enthusiasm and hustle Steve and his teammates showed on the court gained them 62 wins out of the 82 games. Steve led the league with an average of 11 assists per game and was given the NBA's Most Valuable Player award for the season. This marked the first time a Canadian had won the award. Steve was also picked to play in the all-star game again.

At the Top of His Game

Steve was awarded the MVP for a second time in a row in the 2005–2006 season. He is one of only eight players to have done this. Steve almost won MVP a third time in 2006–2007. He led the league in assists for a third straight year, becoming the first Phoenix Sun in team history to average 11 or more assists in three seasons. In the 2008–2009 season, Steve became the only player in NBA history to shoot 50 percent from the field, 40 percent from the three-point, and 90 percent from the free-throw in three consecutive seasons. Steve celebrated ranking seventh for NBA career three-pointers in the 2010–2011 season. But despite all of his accomplishments, Steve has not yet won an NBA championship.

Joining the Lakers

The Phoenix Suns agreed to a sign-and-trade deal with the Lakers. This means the Suns will get four draft picks in place of Steve.

Steve's contract with the Phoenix Suns came to an end after the 2011–2012 season. Many teams, such as New York, Dallas, and Toronto, were fighting to sign a deal with the two-time MVP point guard. In the end, Steve signed a three-year contract for $27 million with the Los Angeles Lakers. Playing for the Lakers allows Steve to stay close to his three children, who live in Phoenix with their mother.

More Than Basketball

Steve Nash is more than just a basketball star. He is a loving father of three, a talented actor and director, a smart business man, and an advocate for helping others.

Family Man

Steve married Alejandra Amarilla in 2005. Their twin daughters Lourdes and Isabella were born in 2004, and their son Matteo was born in 2010. Steve and his wife have since separated. The reason he chose to be traded to the Los Angeles Lakers was to live closer to his children, who live in Arizona with their mother.

Getting in Shape

Steve recognizes the importance of exercise for a happy and healthy lifestyle. He began a company called Steve Nash Enterprises, which has invested in nine businesses that center around health, sports, and fitness. In 2007, the company helped create the first Steve Nash Sports Club in Vancouver. It wlater joined with Fitness World to become Steve Nash Fitness World, a popular chain of 17 clubs in British Columbia.

Steve and his daughters are shown sharing some family time in New York.

Helping Others

Steve has always believed in helping others. In 2001, he formed the Steve Nash Foundation. The goal of the organization is to help kids who are in need of health care, personal development, education, and recreation opportunities. Steve's sister Joann helps run the charity. The Steve Nash Foundation is active in several countries around the world, including the United States, Canada, Paraguay, and Uganda. In Steve's home province of British Columbia, the Steve Nash Foundation supports youth basketball organizations. It also works to end child abuse and funds hospital improvements in Paraguay. One of the most popular fundraising events for the Steve Nash Foundation is the Charity Classic basketball game. Steve and other athletes and celebrities get together to play a game of basketball to raise money for the foundation.

ON SCREEN

Steve has appeared in a number of TV shows, movies, and commercials as himself. You can see him in movies such as *Like Mike* and *Life as We Know It*.

He Said It

"I started this Foundation because I really felt the need to try to help people. As a professional athlete, you are in a position and given the opportunity to really have an impact on more than just your immediate surroundings. For me to be able to do that is something that's sometimes challenging, but always worthwhile."
—Message From Steve on the Steve Nash Foundation website

Behind the Camera

Signing with the L.A. Lakers brought another perk for Steve. It gave him the opportunity to live in a city that is at the center of the film industry. After his three-year contract with the Lakers ends, Steve intends to pursue another passion of his—filmmaking. He hopes to work more on Meathawk, the production company he runs with his cousin. Meathawk has produced ads for Nike, vitaminwater®, Toyota, and EA Sports®.

PELÉ

Meathawk is currently working on a new film called *Pelé*. It's a documentary about the Brazilian soccer star and is scheduled to come out in 2014 before the World Cup in Brazil.

Into The Wind

Meathawk's debut film *Into The Wind* was a **documentary** about the life of Canadian icon Terry Fox. In 1980, after losing one of his legs to cancer, Terry decided to embark on a cross-Canada run to raise awareness and funds in the fight against cancer. It was called the Marathon of Hope. Unfortunately, Terry's cancer returned and he was unable to finish his run. He passed away the following year. Terry's efforts are remembered worldwide and hundreds of millions of dollars have been raised in his name since.

He Said It

"I'd like to play three more years and then get more involved in some of these other pursuits, most notably my production company. It is something I spend a lot of time on."
—*Forbes* magazine interview (2012)

Timeline

1974: Born Feb. 7 in Johannesburg, South Africa

1976: Moves to Canada with his family

1992: Wins provincial championships with St. Michaels Blue Jags

1996: Graduates from Santa Clara University School with degree in sociology

1996: First-round NBA Draft pick for Phoenix Suns

1998: Traded to Dallas Mavericks

2000: Leads Canada's men's basketball team at Summer Olympic Games in Sydney, Australia

2001: Forms the Steve Nash Foundation

2002: First time selected for NBA all-star game

2004: Signs with the Phoenix Suns again

2004: Twin daughters Lourdes and Isabella are born

2005: Marries Alejandra Amarilla

2005: NBA MVP for the first time

2005: Leads NBA in assists for the first time

2006: NBA MVP for second year in a row

2006: Leads NBA in assists for second year in a row

2006: Chosen as one of *Time Magazine*'s 100 people who shape our world

2007: Leads NBA in assists for third year in a row

2008: Reaches 1,300 career three-pointers

2010: Seventh on NBA's all-time three-pointers list

2010: Leads NBA in assists for the fourth time

2010: Son Matteo is born

2010: Production company Meathawk releases film *Into The Wind*

2010: Torchbearer for Canada at 2010 Winter Olympic Games opening ceremonies

2011: Leads the NBA in assists for the fifth time

2012: Signs with the Los Angeles Lakers

2012: Profiled by *Forbes* magazine in Celebrity 100 issue

2012: Eighth time chosen for NBA all-star game

2014: Film *Pelé* scheduled to be released

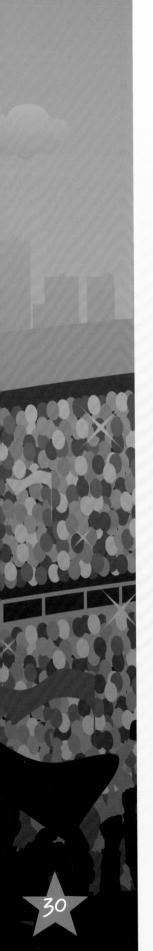

Glossary

apartheid The system of segregation in South Africa

assist A pass made to a teammate who then scores

documentary A movie or TV show about real events or a real person or people

draft The choosing of new players by teams in the NBA

lineup The players of a team on the court at one time

NBA Short for National Basketball Association, a professional basketball league in North America

NCAA Short for National Collegiate Athletic Association

NHL Short for National Hockey League, a professional ice hockey league in North America

perks Short for "perquisites"; privileges

point guard The player who directs his team's offense

rebound Taking possession of a ball after a missed shot

Find Out More

Books

Rud, Jeff. *Steve Nash*: *The Making of an MVP*.
   Puffin Canada 2007.

Arseneault, Paul, and Peter Assaff. *Steve Nash*.
   Heritage House, 2010.

Savage, Jeff. *Steve Nash* (Amazing Athletes).
   Lerner Publications, 2007.

Websites

NBA profile of Steve Nash's career scoring statistics
   http://www.nba.com/playerfile/steve_nash/

Steve Nash Fitness World & Sports Club
   www.fitnessworld.ca/

Steve Nash Foundation
   https://stevenash.org

Index

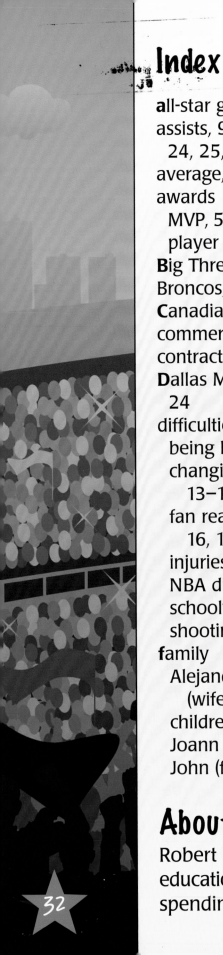

About the Author

Robert Walker is an author of popular educational books for young readers. He enjoys spending time with his wife and small dogs.